TIME
FOR KIDS

PRESIDENT

OBAMA

A Day in the Life of America's Leader

TIME
FOR KIDS

PRESIDENT
OBAMA

A DAY IN THE LIFE OF
AMERICA'S LEADER

PRODUCED BY:

DOWNTOWN
BOOKWORKS INC.

President:	Julie Merberg
Writer and Photo Researcher:	Sarah Parvis

Special Thanks: Patty Brown, Pam Abrams, LeeAnn Pemberton, Steve Levine, Jeanette Leardi, Brian Michael Thomas, Amanda Culp, Morris Katz

DESIGNED BY:	mouse+tiger

TIME FOR KIDS

Managing Editor:	Nellie Gonzalez Cutler
Editor, Time Learning Ventures:	Jonathan Rosenbloom

TIME INC. HOME ENTERTAINMENT

Publisher:	Richard Fraiman
General Manager:	Steven Sandonato
Executive Director, Marketing Services:	Carol Pittard
Director, Retail & Special Sales:	Tom Mifsud
Director, New Product Development:	Peter Harper
Assistant Director, Bookazine Marketing:	Laura Adam
Assistant Publishing Director, Brand Marketing:	Joy Butts
Associate Counsel:	Helen Wan
Design & Prepress Manager:	Anne-Michelle Gallero
Book Production Manager:	Susan Chodakiewicz
Brand Manager:	Shelley Rescober

Special Thanks: Christine Austin, Glenn Buonocore, Jim Childs, Jacqueline Fitzgerald, Rasanah Goss, Lauren Hall, Jennifer Jacobs, Suzanne Janso, Brynn Joyce, Robert Marasco, Amy Migliaccio, Brooke Reger, Ilene Schreider, Adriana Tierno, Alex Voznesenskiy, Sydney Webber, Jonathan White

2009 © Time Inc. Home Entertainment

Published by TIME FOR KIDS Books

Time Inc.
1271 Avenue of the Americas
New York, New York 10020

ISBN 13: 978-1-60320-829-1
ISBN 10: 1-60320-829-1

TIME FOR KIDS is a trademark of Time Inc.

We welcome your comments and suggestions about TIME FOR KIDS Books. Please write to us at:
TIME FOR KIDS Books
Attention: Book Editors
PO Box 11016
Des Moines, IA 50336-1016

If you would like to order any of our hardcover Collector's Edition books, please call us at 1-800-327-6388.
(Monday through Friday, 7:00 a.m.—8:00 p.m. or Saturday, 7:00 a.m.—6:00 p.m. Central Time).

CONTENTS

1

THE ROAD TO THE WHITE HOUSE

FROM HONOLULU, HAWAII, to Washington, D.C.,
Barack Obama's journey to the White House has included stops in
Indonesia, Chicago, Harvard Law School, the United States Senate,
and many other interesting places. Read on to learn more about the
President's life, the election process, and the Obama family's first
days as our nation's First Family.

BEFORE THE PRESIDENCY

1967 Barack Obama travels to Indonesia, where he spends four years with his mother and her second husband.

1971 He returns to Hawaii and begins living with his grandparents, Stanley and Madelyn Dunham.

1970s

1960s

Barack Obama's mother, **Ann Dunham**, was born and raised in Kansas. His father, Barack Obama Sr., came from Kenya, a country in West Africa.

August 4, 1961 Barack Obama is born in Honolulu, Hawaii.

TIME for Fun

During his time in Indonesia, young Barack Obama lived in the country's capital, Jakarta. The first house he lived in did not have a flush toilet, and the streets in the neighborhood were not yet paved. While there, his stepfather, Lolo Soetoro, gave him a pet ape named Tata. Barack Obama also tried cool new foods such as snake meat and roasted grasshopper!

The **Obama family** waits for the results of the 2004 U.S. Senate election.

Barack Obama and his grandparents celebrate his graduation from high school in 1979.

2004 He gives an important speech at the Democratic National Convention and becomes well known. Three months later, he is elected to the U.S. Senate from Illinois.

1990 Barack Obama becomes the first African-American president of the *Harvard Law Review*, a respected publication.

2002 Barack Obama is reelected to the Illinois State Senate.

1996 He runs for a seat in the Illinois State Senate and wins.

1981–83 He goes to Columbia University in New York City, majoring in political science.

2000s

1990s

1980s

1988 He begins Harvard Law School. After his first year, he spends a summer working for a top law firm in Chicago, where he meets Michelle Robinson.

1985 Barack Obama moves to Chicago to work as a community organizer.

1991 He graduates from Harvard Law School and returns to Chicago.

1998 Malia Ann Obama is born. Barack Obama is reelected to the state senate.

2000 He runs for a seat in the U.S. House of Representatives and loses.

2001 Sasha Obama is born. Her full name is Natasha.

Barack Obama and **Michelle Robinson** marry in 1992.

Barack Obama hangs out between classes at Harvard Law School.

He's in the Running!

On February 10, 2007, U.S. Senator Barack Obama announced that he was running for the presidency. As a 45-year-old first-term U.S. Senator, he was an unlikely candidate. He was young and relatively inexperienced.

In his announcement, Barack Obama acknowledged his lack of experience. He told the crowd:

"I know I haven't spent a lot of time learning the ways of Washington, but I've been there long enough to know that the ways of Washington must change."

For the location of his announcement, Barack Obama chooses the steps of Chicago's Old State Capitol building in Springfield, Illinois. President Abraham Lincoln gave an important speech there in 1858.

THE ROAD TO THE CONVENTION

THE ANNOUNCEMENT

First a candidate must announce that he or she is running for President. To do so, a person must be a natural-born U.S. citizen at least 35 years old. He or she must have lived in the U.S. for at least 14 years.

THE RACE BEGINS

Several Democratic party candidates and several Republican party candidates compete against one another for the support of their party's **delegates**. Delegates are members of the Democratic and Republican parties who promise their support to a candidate. The candidate with the support of the most delegates wins his or her party's nomination.

VOTERS WEIGH IN

To help decide which candidate from each party will win the party's nomination, states hold gatherings to find out which candidate the people support. Some states hold primary elections. Others hold what is known as a caucus.

PRIMARY ELECTIONS

Primary elections, or "the primaries," are similar to general elections, except in most states, people may only vote for candidates or delegates from their own political party.

CAUCUSES

A **caucus** is a gathering where party leaders and citizens get together, discuss the issues and candidates, and then cast their votes. Caucus rules vary from party to party and from state to state.

AND THE NOMINEE IS. . .

Primary elections and caucuses help to determine which candidate each delegate will support. In the Democratic party, there are 4,234 delegates. A candidate needs 2,118 delegate votes to secure the nomination.

Barack Obama's main Democratic rival was U.S. Senator Hillary Clinton. They both campaigned hard, and by June 3, 2008, Barack Obama had won 2,201 delegates to Hillary Clinton's 1,896. Hillary Clinton was out of the race the next day.

Joe Biden was introduced as Barack Obama's running mate on the final night of the 2008 Democratic National Convention.

Thousands of members of each party attend the conventions, where they whip up excitement for the upcoming election.

THE CAMPAIGN TRAIL

THE CONVENTION

In the summer of a presidential election year, both parties gather their members for a national convention. The delegates from each party cast their ballots for their nominee. The 2008 Democratic National Convention was held in Denver, Colorado, from August 25 to August 28. After exciting speeches by Michelle Obama, Hillary Clinton, former President Bill Clinton, and other important politicians, Barack Obama was formally named the Democratic party's candidate for the presidency.

Democratic nominee
Barack Obama and
Republican nominee
John McCain take part
in a televised debate.

THE NOMINEES CAMPAIGN... AND CAMPAIGN... AND CAMPAIGN

In the few months between the national conventions and the general election, Democrat Barack Obama and Republican Senator John McCain traveled the country giving speeches, raising money, and telling voters what they would do if they became President.

AND THE WINNER IS...

While campaigning, Barack Obama spoke about changing energy policies, improving the health-care system, cutting taxes for many Americans, and creating more affordable housing, among other issues. He also used the Internet to campaign. By Election Day, his campaign had an e-mail list of about 13 million addresses. Americans responded to Barack Obama's message of hope and change, and he became the 44th President of the United States.

Seven-year-old Sasha and 10-year-old Malia Obama join their parents onstage at an election night celebration in Chicago.

DID YOU KNOW?

Barack Obama took the oath of office using the same Bible that Abraham Lincoln used when he was sworn in as President on March 4, 1861.

14

Becoming President

ELECTION DAY!

Every election year, votes are cast on the Tuesday following the first Monday in November. On Tuesday, November 4, 2008, 63.6% of all voters went to the polls.

THE ELECTORAL COLLEGE

When voters cast their ballots for a candidate on Election Day, it is as if they are voting for groups of electors rather than a particular candidate. These electors actually choose the President. Each state has a number of electors equal to the number of senators and representatives it has. Washington, D.C., also has three electors. In nearly every state, all of the electors must vote for the party that won the most votes. To win the presidency, a candidate must receive at least 270 of the 538 possible electoral votes. Barack Obama won 365 electoral votes to become President of the United States.

THE OATH OF OFFICE

On Inauguration Day, the country's new leader takes the oath of office and becomes President. He or she states the presidential oath:

> *"I do solemnly swear (or affirm) that I will faithfully execute the office of President of the United States, and will to the best of my ability, preserve, protect, and defend the Constitution of the United States."*

INAUGURAL ADDRESS

On January 20, 2009, Barack Obama became the first African-American President in U.S. history. After reciting the oath of office, the new President delivered his inaugural speech. Though it was a cold winter day, millions of visitors flooded the nation's capital, and millions more tuned in to TVs, radios, and computers worldwide to witness the historic event.

U.S. PRESIDENTS

Upon taking the presidential oath of office, Barack Obama joined a list of 42 other men who held the job before him. Here are the men who have been elected to America's highest office.

1. George Washington
1789–1797

2. John Adams
1797–1801

3. Thomas Jefferson
1801–1809

4. James Madison
1809–1817

5. James Monroe
1817–1825

6. John Quincy Adams
1825–1829

7. Andrew Jackson
1829–1837

8. Martin Van Buren
1837–1841

9. William Henry Harrison
1841

10. John Tyler
1841–1845

11. James K. Polk
1845–1849

12. Zachary Taylor
1849–1850

13. Millard Fillmore
1850–1853

14. Franklin Pierce
1853–1857

15. James Buchanan
1857–1861

16. Abraham Lincoln
1861–1865

17. Andrew Johnson
1865–1869

18. Ulysses S. Grant
1869–1877

19. Rutherford B. Hayes
1877–1881

20. James A. Garfield
1881

21. Chester A. Arthur
1881–1885

22. Grover Cleveland*
1885–1889

23. Benjamin Harrison
1889–1893

24. Grover Cleveland*
1893–1897

25. William McKinley
1897–1901

26. Theodore Roosevelt
1901–1909

27. William H. Taft
1909–1913

28. Woodrow Wilson
1913–1921

29. Warren G. Harding
1921–1923

30. Calvin Coolidge
1923–1929

31. Herbert Hoover
1929–1933

32. Franklin D. Roosevelt
1933–1945

33. Harry S Truman
1945–1953

34. Dwight D. Eisenhower
1953–1961

35. John F. Kennedy
1961–1963

36. Lyndon B. Johnson
1963–1969

37. Richard M. Nixon
1969–1974

38. Gerald Ford
1974–1977

39. Jimmy Carter
1977–1981

40. Ronald Reagan
1981–1989

41. George H.W. Bush
1989–1993

42. Bill Clinton
1993–2001

43. George W. Bush
2001–2008

44. Barack Obama
2008–

*Grover Cleveland is the only President who served two terms that were not back to back.

The **Pentagon** is the headquarters of the U.S. Department of Defense. It is huge! More than 26,000 people work there.

The **Lincoln Memorial** pays tribute to Abraham Lincoln, President during the Civil War.

The **Jefferson Memorial** honors President Thomas Jefferson, one of the main authors of the Declaration of Independence.

The **Washington Monument** is 555 feet (169 m) tall. Built between 1848 and 1884, it honors President George Washington.

The **National Mall** is the grassy area between the Capitol and the Lincoln Memorial and between the White House and the Jefferson Memorial. This lawn is surrounded by many museums, including the National Gallery of Art, the National Museum of Natural History, and the National Air and Space Museum.

WELCOME TO WASHINGTON, D.C.

After winning the general election, the Obama family packed up their belongings and moved from Chicago to Washington, D.C. The nation's capital, also known as the District of Columbia, is home to many museums, memorials, monuments, and landmarks.

The **Vietnam Veterans Memorial** features a wall with the names of more than 58,000 Americans who died during the Vietnam War.

The **White House** is here!

The **National Archives Building** holds original copies of the Declaration of Independence, the Constitution, and the Bill of Rights.

The **Capitol** is where members of the House of Representatives and the Senate meet.

The **Supreme Court Building** is home to the highest court in the land. The nine justices who make up the Supreme Court decide whether laws are constitutional.

Irish immigrant James Hoban won a contest to design the President's home in Washington. He modeled the building after Leinster House in Dublin, which is now where the Irish Parliament meets.

In 1814, British troops set fire to the White House. Afterward, only the outside walls remained standing. Between 1814 and 1817, the mansion was rebuilt. Here it is in 1846.

WELCOME TO THE WHITE HOUSE

Like other First Families before them, the Obamas moved into the White House on Inauguration Day. Ninety-three busy members of the White House staff had about five hours to remove the last of the Bush family's belongings and unload and unpack the Obamas' things. The workers included carpenters, painters, decorators, florists, and others. When the Obamas returned from the Inaugural Parade around 5:00 P.M., they were officially home.

PAST PRESIDENTS

Although George Washington supervised the building of the White House, he never got to live there. **John Adams** moved into the presidential mansion on November 1, 1800, while it was still under construction. First Lady Abigail Adams hung the family's laundry to dry in the East Room.

This side of the building is the West Wing, where many members of the senior staff work. Here, the President works in the Oval Office. The Roosevelt Room, Cabinet Room, and the Press Briefing Room are all in the West Wing.

The main section of the White House is known as the Executive Residence.

The office of the First Lady is in the East Wing. Many social events are planned in the offices here. The White House theater is also in the East Wing.

There are a lot of fun things for the First Family to do on the White House grounds. For example, they can go swimming in the pool. It was installed by Gerald Ford in 1975. There is even an underground passage so members of the First Family can reach the pool without walking across the lawn.

INSIDE THE WHITE HOUSE

Presidents and their families have been living in the White House for more than 200 years. The President's house features 132 rooms, including three kitchens, eight staircases, three elevators, and 35 bathrooms. The rooms are spread over six levels.

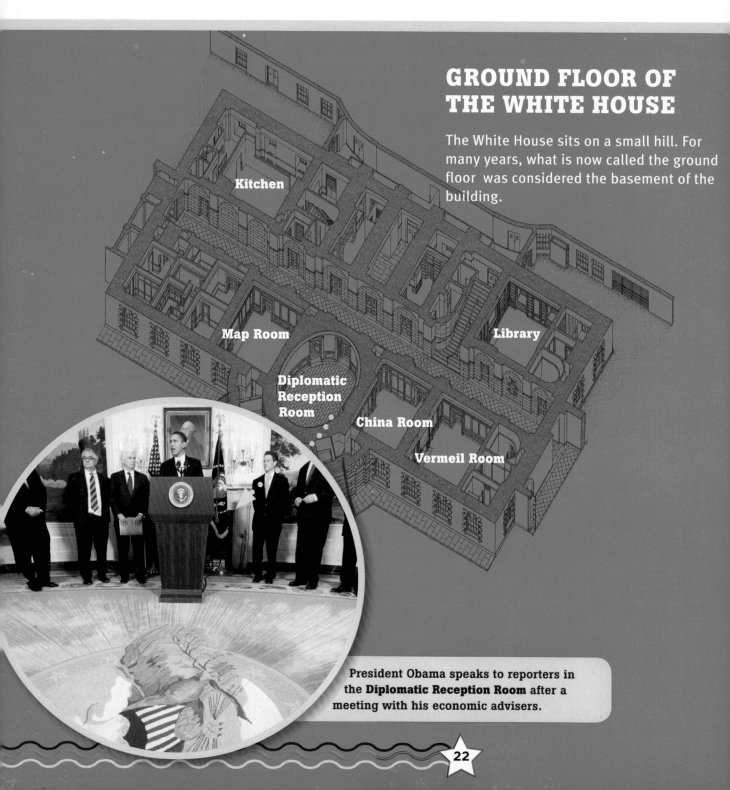

GROUND FLOOR OF THE WHITE HOUSE

The White House sits on a small hill. For many years, what is now called the ground floor was considered the basement of the building.

Kitchen

Map Room

Library

Diplomatic Reception Room

China Room

Vermeil Room

President Obama speaks to reporters in the **Diplomatic Reception Room** after a meeting with his economic advisers.

FIRST FLOOR OF THE WHITE HOUSE

The Obamas greet visitors in the **Blue Room** the day after the Inauguration.

Family Dining Room

State Dining Room

Entrance Hall

Red Room

Blue Room

Green Room

East Room

The President takes part in a town hall meeting in the **East Room**, where he takes questions from audience members and some of the almost 100,000 online participants.

President Obama reads over his notes in the **Red Room** before giving an evening press conference.

2

GOOD MORNING, MR. PRESIDENT

PRESIDENT **O**BAMA may wake up in the master bedroom at the White House. Or he may wake up in a foreign country. He might be catching some shut-eye in the sleeping quarters on Air Force One during an overnight flight. No matter where he is, there are certain things the commander in chief tries to do every morning. In this section, you'll discover some of the things that make up the President's typical morning routine.

EARLY TO RISE

The second and third floors of the White House are the First Family's private quarters. President and Mrs. Obama sleep in the master bedroom on the second floor. President Obama wakes up early, usually around 6:30 A.M. That way he can work out in the White House gym and have breakfast with his family before heading to the Oval Office for work. Michelle Obama is often up at 5:30 A.M. to walk Bo, the family pup, on the South Lawn of the White House.

Good Morning, Malia!
Good Morning, Sasha!

Malia and Sasha have the East and West bedrooms on the second floor of the presidential mansion. The two rooms (which have been home to other First Daughters, including Caroline Kennedy, Amy Carter, and Chelsea Clinton) are connected by a hallway through the rooms' closets. The First Lady believes "Responsibility is something you practice," so Malia and Sasha are responsible for setting their alarm clocks and getting themselves out of bed every morning. And, staff or no staff, First Lady (and Mom in Chief) Michelle Obama expects her daughters to make their own beds!

TIME for Fun

Malia and Sasha had a sleepover with friends on their very first night in the White House. They watched movies, had a scavenger hunt, and got a fantastic shock: a surprise Jonas Brothers concert in their new home!

The President and the First Lady can't always be home in the morning to have breakfast with their girls. Here they take their seats at the National Prayer Breakfast in Washington, D.C.

MORNING WORKOUT

After having breakfast with his family, President Obama likes to hit the gym. Lucky for him, when he is in Washington, he only has to go to the third floor of the White House to find exercise equipment.

Despite his busy schedule, the President squeezes in about 45 minutes of exercise six days a week. "The main reason I work out is to clear my head and relieve stress," he has said. "It's a great way to stay focused."

At the gym, he trades off between lifting weights and doing heart-healthy exercises.

PAST PRESIDENTS

Gerald Ford played football for the University of Michigan and even made it to the national college championships in 1932 and 1933.

President Obama's favorite way to stay in shape is to play basketball.

Michelle Obama works up a sweat tending the White House vegetable garden.

FITNESS IN THE FAMILY

President Obama isn't the only one in the family who likes to keep fit. First Lady Michelle Obama says that if she doesn't work out, she doesn't feel good. Before moving to the White House, Mrs. Obama woke up at 4:30 in the morning to exercise before work. Now she's up at 5: 30 A.M. and at the gym about four times a week. She enjoys all sorts of exercises, such as running on the treadmill, lifting weights, jumping rope, and even kickboxing.

As a family, the Obamas like to take part in other healthful activities such as swimming, riding bikes, walking the family dog, working in the garden, or shooting hoops on the White House basketball court.

DID ★ YOU ★ KNOW?

The First Lady has always been surrounded by basketball lovers. Her older brother, Craig Robinson, is currently the head coach of the men's basketball team at Oregon State University.

GROWING UP
IN THE WHITE HOUSE

Sasha (left) and Malia enjoy
the Inaugural Parade.

The President is extremely happy that he gets to spend time with his daughters most mornings before they go to school. When their father became the 44th President, Malia Ann Obama was 10 years old. Natasha Obama, better known as Sasha, was just 7 years old.

Like kids across the United States, Malia and Sasha go to school and have to do their homework. They like to hang out with their friends and have sleepovers. They play soccer and basketball and take part in clubs at school. They watch *Hannah Montana* and adore the Jonas Brothers. Unlike average kids, though, they live in the most famous house in America with their own mini movie theater and bowling alley. But even if they get to fly on Air Force One and meet some of the most famous people in the world, they still have to go to bed when their mom and dad tell them to.

TIME CAPSULE: FIRST KIDS

Malia and Sasha are not the only young people to enjoy life in the White House. Here are some of the other children who lived at 1600 Pennsylvania Avenue in Washington, D.C.

President Nixon hosted the wedding of his daughter, **Tricia Nixon** at the White House in 1971.

Susan Ford helped her father, President Gerald Ford, with his tie before a White House reception. She said that living in the presidential mansion was "like a fairy tale."

Tad Lincoln, who was 7 years old when Abraham Lincoln became President, liked to run around the White House in a soldier uniform and play war games.

Amy Carter was 9 years old when her parents, Jimmy and Rosalynn Carter, moved to Washington. She famously read a book at the table during a state dinner.

Caroline Kennedy was 4 years old when her father, John F. Kennedy, became President. Her brother, **John Jr.,** was an infant.

President Obama and White House Chief Usher Stephen Rochon walk along the West Colonnade to get to the Oval Office.

OFF TO WORK

I t takes the average American about 25 minutes to get to work. President Obama sure has them beat! To get to his office, he has a 45-second commute on foot. He just needs to get from the second floor of the White House Residence to his office in the West Wing on the first floor. The President often walks outside along the West Colonnade, which gives him a beautiful view of the Rose Garden.

STEPHEN ROCHON

In 1997, after serving in the Coast Guard for 36 years, Stephen Rochon was offered a job at the White House. As White House Chief Usher, it is his job to make the executive mansion run smoothly. Rochon supervises the staff, oversees construction and redecorating projects, is in charge of the kitchen, and keeps track of the mansion's budget.

OFF TO SCHOOL

Malia and Sasha Obama attend Sidwell Friends School, a private school. Malia goes to Sidwell's middle school in Washington, D.C. Sasha is in the lower school in Bethesda, Maryland, which is just outside Washington, D.C.

It is not the first time the school has had members of the Secret Service guarding its doors, or the first time students have seen the Presidential motorcade pull into the parking lot. Children of many important people have attended Sidwell Friends. In fact, three of Vice President Joe Biden's grandchildren go there.

PAST PRESIDENTS

Chelsea Clinton, daughter of former President **Bill Clinton** and current Secretary of State Hillary Clinton, graduated from Sidwell Friends School in 1997. Chelsea was 12 years old when her father became President. Her Secret Service detail referred to her by the code name Energy.

On January 5, 2009, the Obamas get ready for Malia and Sasha's first day at Sidwell Friends School.

HE'S GOT MAIL!

Every morning, the President's staff delivers to him a special purple folder, which contains mail from 10 Americans. In these letters, he reads about the hopes, wishes, concerns, and suggestions of average citizens.

Although Barack Obama is surrounded by an enormous staff who help keep him up to date on everything going on in the country and in the world, reading a batch of letters every morning is a great way for the President to hear directly from voters about what is important to them.

DID ★ YOU ★ KNOW?

President Obama receives more than 40,000 letters a day.

THE WRITE STUFF

The director of the White House Office of Correspondence is Mike Kelleher. Sometimes when Kelleher arrives at his office, he finds hundreds of pieces of mail in boxes piled high against the wall outside his door. Kelleher and his staff sort all of the letters and keep a tally of the subjects covered in the letters. This helps them pick messages about many different topics.

And what makes one letter stand out more than another? "We pick messages that are compelling, things people say that, when you read it, you get a chill," Kelleher says. Most days, President Obama writes back to a few Americans. Sometimes, the letters motivate the President to learn more. He will then ask his staff to look into a particular problem or issue and report back to him.

Mail arrives addressed to everyone who lives in the White House. Even Bo, the family dog, has his own mailbox!

Eighth grader Ty'Sheoma Bethea wrote to Congress, asking lawmakers to help improve her school. Her letter ended up in the hands of President Obama, who was so impressed that he invited her to attend his speech before Congress.

PREPPING FOR THE DAY

Before President Obama arrives in the Oval Office every morning, staff members begin to arrive in the West Wing. Around 7:30 A.M., some of his most senior staff members get together to go over the major events of the day. Chief of Staff Rahm Emanuel, Press Secretary Robert Gibbs, and Senior Advisors David Axelrod, Valerie Jarrett, and Pete Rouse are involved with the President's day-to-day decision making. They make last-minute changes to the President's daily schedule, share information on topics being discussed at the time, and plan for the day.

Senior Advisor **Valerie Jarrett** was born in Iran. She helped Barack Obama build his political career in Chicago but had never worked in Washington when she took the job at the White House.

The President chats with trusted adviser Valerie Jarrett before a morning meeting.

Many members of the President's staff are young. From left to right, Special Assistant Eugene Kang was 24 years old when he began working at the White House. Personal Aide Reggie Love and Personal Secretary Katie Johnson were both 27 years old when they took their jobs.

DAVID AXELROD

Senior Advisor David Axelrod was a journalist for the *Chicago Tribune* newspaper before going into politics. He advised President Obama during both his Senate and presidential campaigns. Axelrod attends the morning economic briefing and other important meetings.

THE GATEKEEPERS

Katie Johnson is President Obama's personal secretary. Along with the President's personal aide, Reggie Love, she has a desk just outside the Oval Office. In addition to coordinating the President's mail and phone calls, she greets many guests, including politicians, world leaders, and celebrities.

Alyssa Mastromonaco keeps President Obama's schedule. She manages a team of 35 people who are responsible for every move the President makes. Mastromonaco generally schedules the President's time in 30- or 45-minute slots. She tries to leave a few minutes between each of his meetings so that he can have "desk time." This allows the President to prepare for meetings or make phone calls.

President-elect Barack Obama announces his picks for two top intelligence offices: Leon Panetta (left) as director of the Central Intelligence Agency and Dennis Blair (right) as director of National Intelligence.

Every morning around 9:30 or 9:45 A.M., President Obama meets with a team of advisers who update him on everything related to the safety and security of the nation. Vice President Biden usually attends the meeting, known as the President's Daily Briefing. Exactly what is discussed inside these top-secret get-togethers is unknown to most people. With the U.S. military in Iraq and Afghanistan, the movements and capabilities of U.S. troops are most likely discussed. Director of National Intelligence Dennis Blair also shares with President Obama information about security threats to the United States. The group probably discusses the best ways to deal with any possible threats.

DID YOU KNOW?

Not all threats come in the form of terrorists or military concerns. The threat of an illness, such as H1N1, or swine flu, is also an issue of national security.

The **Central Intelligence Agency** (CIA) collects intelligence around the globe. The CIA sometimes participates in covert, or secret, missions outside the United States.

The **Federal Bureau of Investigation** (FBI) investigates threats to the country's safety within the United States.

The **Department of Homeland Security** coordinates with national, state, and local law enforcement agencies to keep the country safe.

The **Department of Defense** (DOD) manages four major intelligence organizations, including the **National Security Agency** (NSA), which is responsible for making and breaking codes and for keeping certain information from being read and understood by others.

WHO'S WHO IN THE INTELLIGENCE COMMUNITY?

The director of National Intelligence, Dennis Blair, is in charge of the U.S. Intelligence Community (IC). This job was created in 2004 to coordinate the intelligence activities of 16 different groups. Here are some of the biggest members of the IC.

The **U.S. Coast Guard** is in charge of security in U.S. waters and ports and along the country's coasts.

The **Department of Energy** focuses on threats of nuclear terrorism and sizes up the nuclear capabilities of other countries.

The NSA is in charge of breaking codes to understand secret messages. A **cryptogram** is a kind of code in which each letter of a word is replaced by a different letter. Julius Caesar, a Roman leader who lived more than 2,000 years ago, came up with a code by shifting the alphabet down three places. His code alphabet began with d, e, f instead of a, b, c. Use his alphabet at the right to decode three messages written in the shifted alphabet.

CAESAR'S SHIFTED ALPHABET:

A B C D E F G H I J K L M N O P Q R S T U V W X Y Z
D E F G H I J K L M N O P Q R S T U V W X Y Z A B C

ORRN   RXW   EHKLQG   BRX

_ _ _ _   _ _ _   _ _ _ _ _ _   _ _ _

WRS   VHFUHW

_ _ _   _ _ _ _ _ _

HQWHU   DW   BRXU   RZQ   ULVN

_ _ _ _ _   _ _   _ _ _ _   _ _ _   _ _ _ _

Answers on page 128.

ECONOMIC BRIEFING

Because of the worldwide economic recession in 2008–2009, Barack Obama added a new meeting to his morning routine: the daily economic briefing. Every morning (often around 10:00 A.M.), he meets with a group of economic advisers to get the most up-to-date information on the nation's economy. These meetings are usually private, and held in the Oval Office.

Secretary of the Treasury Timothy Geithner is in charge of the Department of the Treasury, which collects taxes, creates and manages U.S. currency, and oversees national banks. His main role is to protect and strengthen the U.S. economy at home and in other countries.

President Obama receives an economic briefing in the Cabinet Room of the White House.

Vice President Biden joins President Obama for the signing of a law designed to help the economy by saving or creating 3.5 million jobs.

Ben Bernanke is the **chairman of the U.S. Federal Reserve**, which is the central bank of the United States. Known as the Fed, it helps manage the country's money supply, maintain a stable economy, and strengthen the financial standing of the United States.

HELPING THE ECONOMY

The economy is a high priority for President Obama. When he took office, the country was heading into the worst economic crisis since the Great Depression of the 1930s. Nearly 3 million jobs had been lost, and economists predicted many more Americans would soon be out of work. Obama and his chief economic advisers worked with Congress to draft and pass an important piece of legislation designed to help the economy. On January 28, 2009, the President signed the American Recovery and Reinvestment Act, which provided $787 million for projects such as building roads and bridges, investing in more eco-friendly energy sources, upgrading mass transportation, and improving the health-care system.

SENIOR STAFF MEETING

Like other leaders before him, President Obama has chosen several men and women he can turn to for advice. He often meets with this group for 15 or 20 minutes around 10:30 A.M. to discuss the most pressing issues of the day. If the President is giving a speech later in the day or sitting down with people such as lawmakers, members of the auto industry, or groups of teachers, these Oval Office insiders will go over the topics that will be covered in the meetings.

President Obama sits down for a morning meeting with his senior staff, including (left to right): David Axelrod, Jim Messina, Pete Rouse, Rahm Emanuel, Robert Gibbs, Phil Schiliro, Mona Sutphen, Alyssa Mastromonaco, and Valerie Jarrett.

President Obama and Rahm Emanuel chat during a reception in the Blue Room.

THE PRESIDENT'S CHIEF OF STAFF

Barack Obama's chief of staff, Rahm Emanuel, might be the second most powerful person in the U.S. government. Emanuel manages the White House staff and decides who can meet with the President. The role of White House chief of staff changes with each President. In the case of Emanuel, the job carries a lot of influence. He is a close aide to the President and works tirelessly to help the President meet his goals.

Before joining the Obama administration, Emanuel served as a Democratic member of the U.S. House of Representatives. Like Barack Obama, Emanuel was elected by the people of Illinois.

President Obama isn't the only one to work through lunch. Here, First Lady Michelle Obama serves lunch to homeless men and women just blocks away from the White House at Miriam's Kitchen.

LUNCHTIME

More often than not, President Obama's weekday lunches involve work. He generally shares a meal with a senior adviser in the small dining room off the Oval Office. Or he may use the time to meet one-on-one with a member of the House of Representatives or the Senate and discuss upcoming pieces of legislation. When foreign leaders are in town, lunch can be a more formal affair. Sometimes the President attends lunchtime presentations or celebrations, such as the yearly Saint Patrick's Day Lunch.

The President's lunch companions vary from day to day, but once every week, President Obama takes his midday meal with Vice President Biden. They usually meet in a private dining room in the West Wing, and the President chooses the menu.

President Obama and Vice
President Biden enjoy their
weekly lunch at a burger joint in
Arlington, Virginia.

PLEASE DO NOT TAKE A
TABLE BEFORE YOU HAVE
ORDERED AND HAVE A
NUMBER.

PLEASE ASK FOR ASSISTANCE
IN MOVING TABLES.
PLEASE GIVE SEATING
PRIORITY TO OTHERS WHEN
APPROPRIATE

PAST PRESIDENTS

President Reagan also shared
weekly lunches with his Vice
President **George H.W. Bush.**

PRESS CONFERENCE

When major events happen in the United States and elsewhere in the world, the President has to think seriously about how he will respond. He must choose his words carefully because they will be repeated over and over in newspapers, on television, on the radio, and on the Internet throughout the world.

White House Press Secretary Robert Gibbs is the main spokesperson for the Obama administration. He shares the President's comments on events in the news and provides summaries of the President's meetings and conversations with lawmakers, heads of government, and industry leaders.

Press Secretary Gibbs holds press briefings on most days around 1:30 or 2:00 P.M. During press conferences, he makes opening remarks, then takes questions from journalists. To be able to answer all the detailed questions on behalf of the President, he must stay on top of everything going on in the White House.

There are only 49 seats in the White House briefing room. The White House Correspondents' Association (not the President's staff) decides who sits in which treasured seat. The seating chart changes from time to time, but the front row usually remains the same. It includes representatives of the Associated Press, NBC, CBS, ABC, Reuters, and CNN. Between 30 and 60 other reporters stand up during press conferences.

Robert Gibbs was born and raised in Auburn, Alabama. A sports fan like the President, Gibbs played goalie on the North Carolina State University soccer team before going into politics. As a member of the President's team of advisers, he works closely with the President to fine-tune his messages. He is often the last person to speak with the President before the President speaks with reporters or other guests.

WHITEHOUSE.GOV

DID ★ YOU ★ KNOW ?

In addition to holding press briefings and press conferences, President Obama communicates with the public through video addresses every Saturday morning. You can watch them at whitehouse.gov/weekly_address.

Secretary Gibbs holds his afternoon briefings in the James S. Brady Press Briefing Room.

BREAK TIME!

The President's job is a busy and stressful one, so it is a big help that his office and his home are under the same roof. With such a quick commute, he can see his family soon after he wraps up work for the day. He can even take short breaks during the day to visit with his family.

Shortly after taking office, President Obama installed a two-story play set on the South Lawn for his children. With a playground so close to his office, sometimes he can leave his desk and spend a few relaxing minutes hanging out with Malia and Sasha.

The names of every President are etched into the brass plates on this picnic table.

To create this extra-special swing set, the President and First Lady made sure the builders used environmentally responsible and recycled materials. In fact, the tire in the swing was first used in a NASCAR race.

PAST PRESIDENTS

The Obamas are not the first First Family to make kid-friendly additions to the White House grounds. Franklin D. Roosevelt put a slide on the lawn for his grandkids. Caroline and John F. Kennedy Jr. played on an outdoor swing set, and **Amy Carter**, the daughter of President Jimmy Carter, loved to play in a tree house made especially for her.

President Obama and Vice President Biden enjoy a few relaxing minutes on the White House putting green before heading back to work.

The Oval Office is here. President Obama can see the play set from his office window.

FIRST POOCH

The newest addition to the Obama family is a Portuguese water dog named Bo. During the race for the White House, Barack and Michelle Obama did everything in their power to keep life normal for Malia and Sasha. But with all the traveling, campaigning, and newfound attention paid to the family, there was no way their lives weren't turned upside down. To thank the girls for being such good sports through the whole process, their parents promised them a dog after the election.

Since his first day in the White House, Bo has been a hit. The First Lady reports that he's "kind of crazy," that he likes to chew on people's feet, and that he sometimes wakes everyone up playing in the middle of the night. But the First Family isn't complaining. They all like to goof around with the dog and take him on walks around the White House grounds.

First Lady Grace Coolidge had a pet raccoon named Rebecca.

President Gerald Ford's dog, Liberty, spent time in the Oval Office and even attended meetings.

President Benjamin Harrison kept a pet goat on the lawn. Named Old Whiskers, the goat once ran off with Harrison's grandchildren while pulling them in a cart.

Macaroni, the pony belonging to **President John F. Kennedy's** daughter, Caroline, was allowed to roam the White House grounds.

President Theodore Roosevelt kept many pets, including the pony his son Archie rides in this 1903 photo. Roosevelt's other furry friends included a badger, a hyena, and a zebra.

President Warren Harding's dog, Laddie Boy, was famous in his day. Newspapers even published fake interviews with him.

TIME CAPSULE:
PRESIDENTIAL PETS

Many dogs and cats have roamed the halls of the White House. But plenty of other critters have lived there, too. Thomas Jefferson was given two bear cubs by the explorers Meriwether Lewis and William Clark, and John Quincy Adams kept a pet alligator.

BUSY DAYS IN D.C.

TALK ABOUT MULTITASKING! When Barack Obama is in Washington, his schedule is jam-packed from morning till night. He may be on the phone with astronauts (as he is in the photo), spending time with lucky schoolchildren, or meeting with members of Congress—or doing all three at the same time. In this section, you'll learn more about the many things that keep the commander in chief occupied when he's in our nation's capital.

3

CAPITAL DAYS

President Obama's schedule varies every day. When he is in Washington, D.C., though, there are a few regularly scheduled events on his daytime agenda, such as his security and economic briefings. Here are a few sample pages from President Obama's appointment book.

FEBRUARY 25, 2009

9:30 A.M. Receive the President's Daily Briefing in Oval Office

10:00 A.M. Receive economic briefing in Oval Office

10:30 A.M. Meet with senior advisers in Oval Office

11:00 A.M. With Vice President Biden, introduce a nominee for Secretary of Commerce in Indian Treaty Room

12:30 P.M. Meet with Vice President Biden and members of the Democratic leadership in Congress in Cabinet Room

3:00 P.M. Meet with Treasury Secretary Geithner and members of the Senate Banking Committee and the House Financial Services Committee in Oval Office

3:45 P.M. Make a statement in Diplomatic Reception Room

7:25 P.M. Host Stevie Wonder performance in East Room

April 21, 2009

9:00 A.M. Receive the President's Daily Briefing in Oval Office

10:00 A.M. Meet one-on-one with King Abdullah of Jordan in Personal Dining Room

10:30 A.M. Hold larger meeting with King Abdullah of Jordan in Oval Office

11:45 A.M. Receive economic briefing in Oval Office

12:15 P.M. Meet with senior advisers in Oval Office

2:00 P.M. Present the Commander in Chief's Trophy to the U.S. Naval Academy football team in Rose Garden

2:45 P.M. Discuss national service with Vice President Biden, Senator Ted Kennedy, and former President Bill Clinton in Oval Office

4:00 P.M. Deliver remarks at the SEED School of Washington, calling on Americans to participate in community activities and work together to improve the nation

Sign the Edward M. Kennedy Serve America Act to expand national service programs

Plant trees with the First Lady at a national park

May 6, 2009

9:45 A.M. Receive President's Daily Briefing in Oval Office

10:05 A.M. Receive economic briefing in Oval Office

10:40 A.M. Meet with senior advisers in Oval Office

11:30 A.M. Meet with Senator Tom Coburn in Oval Office

12:00 P.M. Lunch with Vice President Biden and Senators Max Baucus and Chuck Grassley in Private Dining Room

2:00 P.M. With Vice President Biden, meet with Afghan President Hamid Karzai in Oval Office

2:40 P.M. With Vice President Biden, meet with Pakistani President Asif Ali Zardari in Oval Office

3:30 P.M. With Vice President Biden, hold a trilateral meeting with Presidents Karzai and Zardari in Cabinet Room

4:15 P.M. Deliver remarks in the White House Grand Foyer

THE OVAL OFFICE

President Obama meets with advisers in the Oval Office to discuss the difficult situation in Sudan, a nation in Africa.

When he is in the nation's capital, President Obama spends at least part of his day in the Oval Office. There he meets with government representatives, trusted aides, foreign leaders, and everyday citizens. He makes phone calls, hosts press conferences, and handles much of the day-to-day business of his job.

Each First Family is given a $100,000 allowance to cover redecorating expenses at the White House. Barack and Michelle Obama turned down the money, so the Oval Office looks the same as it did under President George W. Bush. Though the room may look the same, some things are different. President Obama relaxed the dress code in the office, often appearing at work without a suit jacket on. He also turned up the heat. Born and raised in Hawaii, President Obama likes to keep the office warm. Senior Advisor David Axelrod has joked, "You could grow orchids in there." (Orchids are types of flowers often found in tropical areas.)

PAST PRESIDENTS

President William Taft had the first Oval Office built in the White House in 1909. It was destroyed in a fire in 1929, and although it was rebuilt completely, Franklin D. Roosevelt moved the office to its current location in 1933.

TIME CAPSULE:
OVAL OFFICE

Though the 800-square-foot (74-square-meter) room only takes up a small corner of the White House, it has been the scene of many important bill signings, public addresses, and meetings—as well as more casual get-togethers. Here is a look at a few historic and everyday moments in Oval Office history.

Franklin D. Roosevelt signs the declaration of war against Germany on December 11, 1941.

In 1951, a White House staffer delivers a cake for Harry Truman's 67th birthday.

John F. Kennedy gets a Halloween visit from his children in 1963.

In 1963, civil rights leader Martin Luther King Jr. meets with President Lyndon Johnson.

Richard Nixon plays golf with comedian Bob Hope during a 1973 visit.

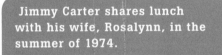

Jimmy Carter shares lunch with his wife, Rosalynn, in the summer of 1974.

Ronald Reagan greets Florida Senator Paula Hawkins in 1987.

On January 22, 2009, the President talks with reporters while signing an executive order to close the U.S. prison at Guantanamo Bay in Cuba within one year.

EXECUTIVE POWERS

Creating laws in the United States requires work by both Congress and the President. But the President can make some decisions without Congress. President Obama has the power to **pardon** people, which means that he can forgive the sentence of a person who has been declared guilty of a federal crime.

He can also issue **executive orders** without the approval of Congress. Executive orders usually clarify or change existing laws. Often a President will use an executive order to make government agencies take action on a particular issue. For example, early in his presidency, Barack Obama signed an order to create the White House Council on Women and Girls, which will be made up of Cabinet secretaries and other senior White House staff. He directed these officials to look into their departments to see what can be done to improve the lives of women and girls.

President Obama poses for a picture with WNBA star Lisa Leslie, who supported the creation of the White House Council on Women and Girls.

CHECKS AND BALANCES

Each branch of the federal government is equally important and has different powers and functions. The legislative branch (Congress) makes laws, the executive branch (the President) carries out those laws, and the judicial branch decides whether those laws are constitutional and legal. This is known as the **separation of powers**. To keep any one branch from having too much power, each branch has the power to regulate the others in some way. This is known as the system of **checks and balances**.

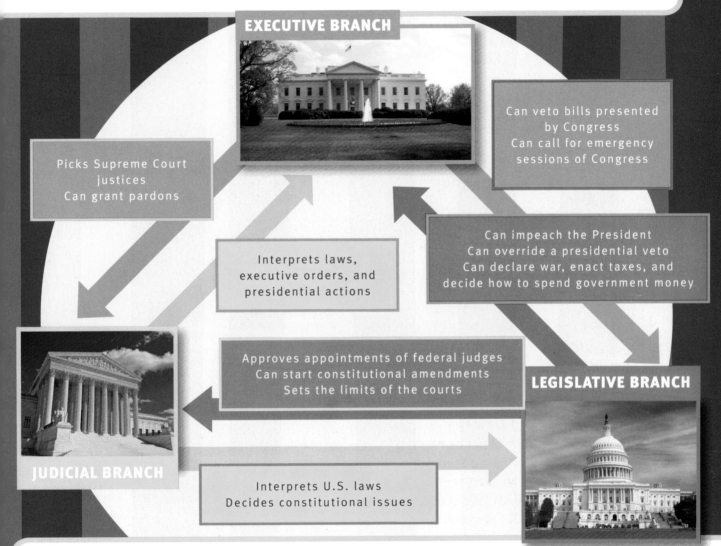

EXECUTIVE BRANCH

Can veto bills presented by Congress
Can call for emergency sessions of Congress

Picks Supreme Court justices
Can grant pardons

Interprets laws, executive orders, and presidential actions

Can impeach the President
Can override a presidential veto
Can declare war, enact taxes, and decide how to spend government money

Approves appointments of federal judges
Can start constitutional amendments
Sets the limits of the courts

LEGISLATIVE BRANCH

JUDICIAL BRANCH

Interprets U.S. laws
Decides constitutional issues

EXECUTIVE ORDERS CAN BE CHECKED

A President can issue an executive order without Congress agreeing, but as part of the system of checks and balances, the judicial branch still has the ability to cancel it. President Harry Truman landed in hot water when he issued an executive order in 1952 that put the federal government in charge of all the country's steel mills. The Supreme Court decided that President Truman was trying to make a law without the approval of Congress and declared this executive order unconstitutional. Since that time, Presidents have usually been more careful about signing executive orders.

President Obama and Vice President Biden take a moment before addressing a group of mayors in February 2009.

THE VICE PRESIDENT

Joe Biden was a senator from Delaware for 36 years before he became the Vice President of the United States. He served on many important committees as a senator, including the Senate Judiciary Committee, which deals with criminal justice, and the Senate Foreign Relations Committee. Many people think President Obama chose him as a running mate for his experience in foreign policy.

As Vice President, Joe Biden helps to run the government. He takes part in important meetings and helps President Obama make decisions about all of the serious issues facing the U.S. When President Obama introduces a measure that he would like made into a law, Vice President Biden uses his experience in Congress to talk with its members and try to win their support. He travels the country sharing the government's message. The Vice President is also the president of the Senate, but he can only cast a vote in the event of a tie (for more, see p. 67).

DID ★ YOU ★ KNOW?

Until 1804, the person who became Vice President was the presidential candidate with the second most electoral votes.

ORDER OF PRESIDENTIAL SUCCESSION

Here is the order of government officials next in line to run the country if the President dies, is too ill to serve, or has been removed from office.

VICE PRESIDENT Joe Biden

SPEAKER OF THE HOUSE Nancy Pelosi

PRESIDENT PRO TEMPORE OF THE SENATE Robert C. Byrd

SECRETARY OF STATE Hillary Rodham Clinton

SECRETARY OF THE TREASURY Timothy Geithner

SECRETARY OF DEFENSE Robert Gates

ATTORNEY GENERAL Eric Holder

SECRETARY OF THE INTERIOR Ken Salazar

SECRETARY OF AGRICULTURE Tom Vilsack

SECRETARY OF COMMERCE Gary Locke

SECRETARY OF LABOR Hilda Solis

SECRETARY OF HEALTH AND HUMAN SERVICES Kathleen Sebelius

SECRETARY OF HOUSING AND URBAN DEVELOPMENT Shaun Donovan

SECRETARY OF TRANSPORTATION Ray LaHood

SECRETARY OF ENERGY Stephen Chu

SECRETARY OF EDUCATION Arne Duncan

SECRETARY OF VETERANS AFFAIRS Eric Shinseki

SECRETARY OF HOMELAND SECURITY Janet Napolitano

DID YOU KNOW?

Four Vice Presidents went on to be elected President: John Adams, Thomas Jefferson, Martin Van Buren, and George H.W. Bush.

VICE PRESIDENTS WHO HAVE MOVED UP

Vice Presidents of the United States have become President nine times.

PRESIDENT	SUCCESSOR	REASON	YEAR
William Henry Harrison	John Tyler	Died	1841
Zachary Taylor	Millard Fillmore	Died	1850
Abraham Lincoln	Andrew Johnson	Assassinated	1865
James Garfield	Chester Arthur	Assassinated	1881
William McKinley	Theodore Roosevelt	Assassinated	1901
Warren Harding	Calvin Coolidge	Died	1923
Franklin Roosevelt	Harry Truman	Died	1945
John F. Kennedy	Lyndon Johnson	Assassinated	1963
Richard Nixon	Gerald Ford	Resigned after being impeached	1974

VISITING THE U.S. CAPITOL

President Obama frequently meets with congressmen and congresswomen. He meets with senators one-on-one or in committees to discuss possible laws or to drum up support for a bill that he would like passed. Other times, he joins them for bill-signing ceremonies or other public events. Members of the House and the Senate meet in the U.S. Capitol, but in different areas of the building. Sometimes, they all get together for joint sessions of Congress. The President does not always attend these sessions, but they can be a good opportunity for him to address all members of Congress at once.

President Obama greets his audience in the chamber of the House of Representatives at the Capitol after delivering his February 24, 2009, address before the joint session of Congress.

THE CAPITOL BUILDING

The Senate Chamber is on the north side of the Capitol building.

The Cha[...]
House of R[...]
is on the s[...]
Capito[...]

WANT TO RUN FOR CONGRESS?

For a person to run for the House of Representatives or the Senate, he or she must meet certain requirements.

U.S. HOUSE OF REPRESENTATIVES*
Must be at least 25 years old

Must be a U.S. citizen for at least 7 years

Must live in the state where he or she is elected

*Members serve for two years

U.S. SENATE**
Must be at least 30 years old

Must be a U.S. citizen for at least 9 years

Must live in the state where he or she is elected

**Members serve for six years

CONGRESS

President Obama frequently meets with members of Congress, or the legislature. The legislative branch of the U.S. government is responsible for drafting the country's laws.

In the United States, the legislature has a **bicameral** structure. This means there are two chambers, the House of Representatives and the Senate. Membership in the House of Representatives is based on the population of each state. There are 435 members of the House.

The political party with more members in either house of Congress is known as the **majority party**. The party with fewer members is called the **minority party**. There are several important legislators who help to keep the House and the Senate running smoothly.

The second most powerful position in the House of Representatives is the Majority Leader. The Majority Leader schedules when bills will be introduced and discussed. He or she also talks to the members of his or her party to make sure they support or oppose bills as a group. Democratic Congressman **Steny Hoyer** of Maryland is currently the **House Majority Leader**.

Whipping Up Support

In each house of Congress, there are two party whips who work to "whip up" support for legislation before it is voted on. Also known as assistant leaders of each house, whips are in charge of counting votes and increasing support within their parties. There is one for the majority party and one for the minority party in each house of Congress.

HERE ARE THE FOUR WHIPS IN CONGRESS.

HOUSE	POSITION	NAME	STATE REPRESENTED
U.S. House of Representatives	Majority Whip	**Jim Clyburn (Dem.)**	South Carolina
U.S. House of Representatives	Minority Whip	**Eric Cantor** (Rep.)	Virginia
U.S. Senate	Majority Whip	Dick Durbin (Dem.)	Illinois
U.S. Senate	Minority Whip	Jon Kyl (Rep.)	Arizona

The most powerful member of the minority party in the House is the Minority Leader. This person helps to develop strategies for the Republicans in the House of Representatives and communicates the party's policies to rest of the world. **John Boehner**, a Republican from Ohio, is currently **House Minority Leader.**

President Obama meets with the leaders of both houses of Congress.

Every two years, the members of the majority party in the House of Representatives elect a leader who is known as the **Speaker of the House**. The Speaker of the House is both the leader of the majority party in the House and the leader of the entire House of Representatives. The Speaker calls sessions to order, gives the oath of office to new members, runs debates, and maintains order in the House. The current Speaker of the House is Democrat **Nancy Pelosi** of California.

The **Senate Majority Leader** serves as a spokesperson for the majority party and works with party members to get legislation passed. **Democrat Harry Reid** of Nevada is the current Senate Majority Leader.

President Obama confers with Senator Harry Reid about economic issues before speaking with reporters at the White House.

THE SENATE

Unlike in the House of Representatives, each of the 50 U.S. states gets equal representation in the Senate. There are 100 members, two for each state. Elections for the Senate are staggered so that about one-third of the Senate is elected every two years.

Like members of the House, members of the Senate write, debate, and vote on laws before they present them to the President for his final signature. Senators have many other duties, including ratifying, or approving, treaties drafted by the President and voting to accept or reject presidential nominees to the U.S. Supreme Court, the Cabinet, and other important positions in the government. The Senate also conducts trials of government officials who have been impeached, or charged with a crime, by the House of Representatives.

The **Senate Minority Leader** works for the interests of his or her fellow party members. Kentucky Republican **Mitch McConnell** has been the Minority Leader in the Senate since November 2008.

SENATE PRESIDENT

According to the U.S. Constitution, the Vice President can cast a vote in the Senate only when there is a tie. This doesn't happen often. John Adams, George Washington's second in command from 1789–97, cast 29 tie-breaking votes, the most of any Vice President.

In the Vice President's absence, the **president pro tempore** is in charge of the Senate chamber. (*Pro tempore* means "for the time being," or temporarily, in Latin.) If the president pro tempore cannot be present in the Senate, he or she picks another senator to preside temporarily in his or her place.

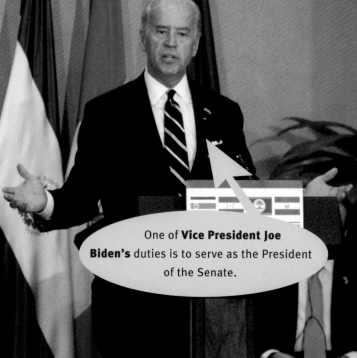

One of **Vice President Joe Biden's** duties is to serve as the President of the Senate.

Robert Byrd, seen here with Defense Secretary Robert Gates, has been the president pro tempore since January 2007. He first held the position from 1989 to 1994, then again from 2001 to 2002.

Lawmakers look on as President Obama signs a bill into law.

SIGNING BILLS INTO LAWS

O ne of the President's biggest jobs is to decide which bills will become laws. Just nine days after taking the presidential oath of office, Barack Obama signed his first bill into law. On January 29, 2009, he put his signature on the Lily Ledbetter Fair Pay Restoration Act, a law designed to make it easier for people who feel they are victims of pay discrimination to sue their employers.

The President has signed many bills, such as the Children's Health Insurance Program bill, which gives health insurance benefits to millions of children from low-income families. He has also okayed laws to protect the U.S. wilderness and to stop the export of the dangerous chemical mercury.

TIME for Fun

SIGNING AND SOUVENIRS

Presidents usually use many different pens when signing new laws. These pens are then handed out as souvenirs, often to the sponsors of the bill and others who worked hard for its passage. "I've been practicing signing my name very slowly," President Obama joked before using 11 different pens to sign his first law.

TO VETO OR NOT TO VETO

The President doesn't sign every law that comes across his desk. Here is what can happen to a bill in Washington.

> A bill can begin in either the House of Representatives or the Senate.

> Once both houses have debated a bill and decided to pass it, the bill ends up on the President's desk.

> The President has two choices.

> He can sign the bill, making it a law.

> He can veto, or refuse to approve, the measure. If the President vetoes a bill, Congress has three choices.

> Congress can rework the bill and send it back to the White House.

> Congress can drop the bill entirely.

> Congress can vote to override the presidential veto. If a two-thirds majority of the house that originally sponsored the bill votes to override the veto, the bill becomes a law.

PAST PRESIDENTS

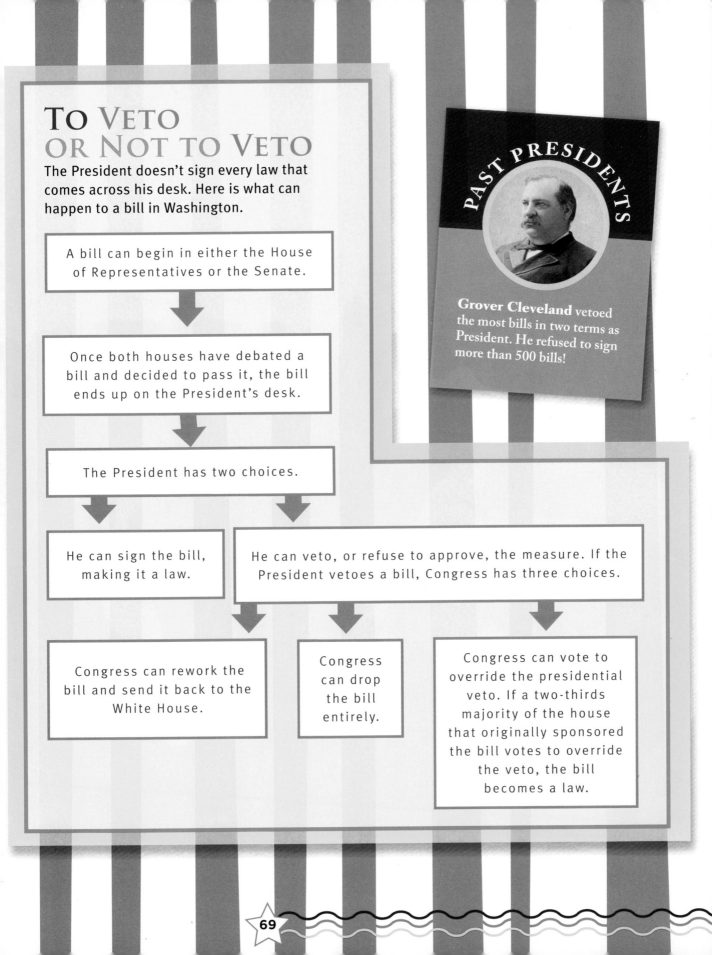

Grover Cleveland vetoed the most bills in two terms as President. He refused to sign more than 500 bills!

MEETING THE PEOPLE

The President's daytime schedule is often full of meetings with Cabinet secretaries, legislators, foreign leaders, and others. But he makes sure to find time to connect with people outside of government as well. Sometimes, individual citizens or groups are invited to the Oval Office to meet with the President. Other times, the White House holds public events like the Easter Egg Roll that allow the President to meet the people he represents. The President also likes to chat with families when he is away from the White House.

After playing basketball in Fort McNair in Washington, D.C., President Obama takes time to talk with families.

The Easter Egg Roll!

One of the largest public events at the White House every year is the Easter Egg Roll. "This is one of the greatest White House traditions because it reminds us that this is the people's house," President Obama said.

Because the Obama administration wants to encourage kids to keep active and stay healthy, the theme of the 2009 event was "Let's Play." Children hunted for eggs hidden around the grounds, played soccer, danced, did yoga, and learned from the White House chefs about healthful snacks. The President even invited families to join him on the basketball court to shoot some hoops. In a storytelling area, honored guests read books to the crowd. Michelle Obama and her mother, Marian Robinson, took turns reading *If You Give a Mouse a Cookie* by Laura Joffe Numeroff.

President Obama delights his audience by reading *Where the Wild Things Are* by Maurice Sendak.

Families enjoy the 1924 Easter Egg Roll.

DID YOU KNOW?

Since 1878, U.S. Presidents have been inviting families to the White House to celebrate the start of spring with an Easter Egg Roll.

MEETING FOREIGN LEADERS

A s President, Barack Obama is the chief diplomat of the United States. This means he handles U.S. relations with the governments of other countries. He meets with foreign leaders to discuss U.S. policies around the world. He works to maintain solid relationships with foreign countries. Often foreign heads of state will visit Washington, D.C., to speak with President Obama in the Oval Office. The leaders may discuss a particular issue, such as trade relations, or they may come to Washington, D.C., as a public show of support for the United States.

As the head of the most powerful nation in the world, America's leader has a lot of influence with other nations. President Obama can use his powerful position to try to bring nations together in agreement.

President Barack Obama talks with Israeli Prime Minister Benjamin Netanyahu about the situation in the Middle East.

President Obama meets with Russian President Dmitry Medvedev. Afterward, they issue a statement saying that the "Era when our countries viewed each other as enemies is long over."

MAKING TREATIES

President Obama has the power to recognize new nations on behalf of the United States and the power to enter into treaties with other nations. **Treaties** are written agreements between two countries and are often used to end wars or make trade pacts. Though the President can enter into a treaty with another nation, the Senate must ratify, or approve, by a two-thirds majority each treaty negotiated by the President.

PAST PRESIDENTS

The Treaty of Versailles, which ended World War I, was mainly drafted by U.S. President **Woodrow Wilson**, French Prime Minister Georges Clemenceau, and British Prime Minister David Lloyd George. Though President Wilson worked tirelessly on the treaty, the U.S. Senate refused to ratify it.

Senator Hillary
Clinton testifies
before the Senate
Foreign Relations
Committee hearing in
order to be confirmed
as Secretary of State.

CHOOSING A TEAM

President Obama is responsible for nominating people to some of the highest offices in the federal government. He appoints men and women to be in charge of national commissions. He also picks federal judges and ambassadors who represent the United States around the world. When a U.S. Supreme Court justice retires or dies, the President chooses someone to fill the empty seat on the court.

For advice in different areas, the President relies on the counsel of his trusted Cabinet. The Cabinet is made up of 15 department heads, all of whom are nominated by the President. Presidential nominees are questioned by the Senate during confirmation hearings. Each nominee must be confirmed, or approved, by a majority of 51 or more senators.

DID YOU KNOW?

Secretary of Defense Robert Gates was sworn in on December 8, 2006. He is the only member of President Obama's Cabinet who held his post under President George W. Bush as well.

MEET THE CABINET SECRETARIES

Each of the 15 Cabinet departments in the U.S. government has different responsibilities. For more information, go to their Web sites.

DEPARTMENT OF EDUCATION
Secretary Arne Duncan
*develops educational policies and
helps with financial aid
for schooling
ed.gov

**DEPARTMENT OF HOUSING AND
URBAN DEVELOPMENT**
Secretary Shaun Donovan
*supports affordable housing and
community development
hud.gov

DEPARTMENT OF STATE
Secretary Hillary Clinton
*helps to develop foreign policy and
works with other countries
state.gov

DEPARTMENT OF AGRICULTURE
Secretary Tom Vilsack
*supports farmers and healthful
agriculture and food policies
usda.gov

DEPARTMENT OF ENERGY
Secretary Steven Chu
*develops energy policies and looks
into cleaner energy sources
doe.gov

DEPARTMENT OF THE INTERIOR
Secretary Ken Salazar
*protects and preserves natural
resources and wildlife; oversees
national parks
doi.gov

**DEPARTMENT OF
TRANSPORTATION**
Secretary Ray LaHood
*manages plane travel and U.S.
highways, railroads, and shipping ports
dot.gov

DEPARTMENT OF COMMERCE
Secretary Gary Locke
*promotes business and trade within
the country and with other nations
doc.gov

**DEPARTMENT OF HEALTH
AND HUMAN SERVICES**
Secretary Kathleen Sebelius
*works to ensure public health, food
safety, health insurance and assistance
hhs.gov

DEPARTMENT OF JUSTICE
Attorney General Eric Holder
*enforces laws and makes sure all
Americans are treated fairly under the law
usdoj.gov

DEPARTMENT OF THE TREASURY
Secretary Timothy Geithner
*creates U.S. money and handles the
collection of taxes
ustreas.gov

DEPARTMENT OF DEFENSE
Secretary Robert Gates
*in charge of the
U.S. armed forces
defenselink.mil

**DEPARTMENT OF
HOMELAND SECURITY**
Secretary Janet Napolitano
*works to keep the country secure and
to prevent terrorist attacks
dhs.gov

DEPARTMENT OF LABOR
Secretary Hilda Solis
*protects the safety and rights
of workers
dol.gov

DEPARTMENT OF VETERANS AFFAIRS
Secretary Eric Shinseki
*helps veterans and their families
va.gov

President Obama addresses
marines at Camp Lejeune
in North Carolina.

COMMANDER IN CHIEF

As President, Barack Obama is commander in chief of the U.S. armed services, which include the army, navy, air force, coast guard, and marines. The U.S. Constitution says that the President and Congress must work together in wartime. Only Congress has the power to declare war, but the President can send U.S. troops into combat under certain conditions. Congress is also in charge of military spending, but the President has the power to direct troops.

When he took office in 2009, President Obama immediately took charge of the military operations in Iraq and Afghanistan.

DID YOU KNOW?

The United States has not formally declared war since World War II.

ADVISERS, ADVISERS, EVERYWHERE

When the President of the United States makes major decisions about U.S. foreign and military policies, he doesn't do it alone. He relies on the specialized knowledge and experience of his advisers. Here are some of those men and women.

Established in 1947, the National Security Council (NSC) is a group that meets to discuss national security and foreign policy concerns and to provide guidance to the President, Cabinet secretaries, and other senior officials. **National Security Advisor James Jones,** a retired four-star general, is the head of the NSC.

The **Secretary of State** is the President's chief adviser on all foreign affairs. He or she travels throughout the world, negotiating with other countries and promoting U.S. policies. **Hillary Clinton** became Secretary of State in 2009.

The Joint Chiefs of Staff is a group of military leaders who provide guidance to civilian leaders in the government. It is made up of the highest-ranking members of the U.S. armed forces and a chairman and vice chairman who are both appointed by the President. **Admiral Michael Mullen** is the **Chairman of the Joint Chiefs of Staff.**

The **Secretary of Defense** advises the President on all matters relating to the safety and security of the country. He or she also serves as an important link between the President and the leaders of the U.S. military. **Robert Gates** is President Obama's Secretary of Defense.

MAKING SPEECHES

Barack Obama is a talented public speaker. During his Presidential campaign, he traveled constantly, speaking in front of crowds large and small in every state in the Union. Now as President, he speaks in public many times each week. He addresses Congress and speaks at schools, town halls, factories, and businesses. He welcomes world leaders and addresses the American people about issues facing the country.

To keep up with all of his speeches and the wide range of issues he talks about, the White House staff includes a team of speechwriters. They help him to perfect his message and be as clear as possible. Because President Obama has such a way with words, he is closely involved with the writing of his remarks.

These devices may look like nothing more than panes of glass, but they are actually **teleprompters.** They display the words of the President's remarks and keep him from forgetting parts of his speeches when he is in front of audiences.

President Obama speaks to the Turkish parliament in Ankara, Turkey.

Spotlight

JON FAVREAU

Often the speechwriting process begins with the President sharing his thoughts with Chief Speechwriter Jon Favreau. Favreau then takes the words and shapes them into a first draft. The two of them will go back and forth until the President is happy, sometimes making adjustments right up until he walks onstage. Favreau has said his goal is to "tell a story from beginning to end" in every speech.

78

Memorable Lines

Here are some lines from some of President Obama's powerful speeches.

"My parents shared not only an improbable love; they shared an abiding faith in the possibilities of this nation. They would give me an African name, Barack, or 'blessed,' believing that in a tolerant America, your name is no barrier to success. They imagined me going to the best schools in the land, even though they weren't rich, because in a generous America you don't have to be rich to achieve your potential.... I stand here knowing that my story is part of the larger American story, that I owe a debt to all of those who came before me, and that in no other country on Earth is my story even possible."
—Keynote address, Democratic National Convention, July 27, 2004, Boston, Massachusetts

"I have never been so naïve as to believe that we can get beyond our racial divisions in a single election cycle, or with a single candidacy—particularly a candidacy as imperfect as my own. But I have asserted a firm conviction—a conviction rooted in my faith in God and my faith in the American people—that working together we can move beyond some of our old racial wounds, and that in fact we have no choice if we are to continue on the path of a more perfect union."
—Speech on race, March 18, 2008, Philadelphia, Pennsylvania

"But in the unlikely story that is America, there has never been anything false about hope. For when we have faced down impossible odds, when we've been told that we're not ready, or that we shouldn't try, or that we can't, generations of Americans have responded with a simple creed that sums up the spirit of a people: Yes we can."
—Concession speech after losing the New Hampshire primary to Hillary Clinton, January 8, 2008, Nashua, New Hampshire

"There's one rule that lies at the heart of every religion—that we do unto others as we would have them do unto us. This truth transcends nations and peoples—a belief that isn't new; that isn't black or white or brown; that isn't Christian or Muslim or Jew. It's a belief that pulsed in the cradle of civilization, and that still beats in the hearts of billions around the world. It's a faith in other people, and it's what brought me here today."
—Speech on U.S.-Muslim Relations, June 4, 2009, Cairo, Egypt

THE FIRST LADY

The job of the First Lady is not an elected position, but it is an important one. Like the President, First Lady Michelle Obama keeps an extremely busy schedule. She gets up early, walks the family dog (even though Malia and Sasha promised they would walk him!), helps get the girls off to school, and heads to the gym before her many meetings and appearances begin.

Before moving to Washington, D.C., Mrs. Obama worked as a lawyer and a hospital administrator. Now her days are spent working hard as First Lady. She frequently volunteers her time to help others. She speaks to individuals and groups on topics such as workers' rights, the troubles faced by military families, and how to best balance work and parenthood. She meets with government employees to tell them about some of the President's programs and helps to entertain the many influential world leaders that pass through the White House.

DID ★ YOU ★ KNOW ?

As a young girl, Michelle Obama skipped the second grade.

First Lady Michelle Obama speaks with Queen Rania of Jordan in the Yellow Oval Room in the White House.

Mrs. Obama visits a bilingual school in Washington, D.C.

Michelle Obama visits the Cathedral of Notre Dame in Strasbourg, France, with the spouses of other world leaders in April 2009.

TIME for Fun

The First Lady loves to eat comfort foods such as macaroni and cheese, french fries, and barbecue. Sometimes she and members of her staff leave the White House grounds and go out for burgers at local diners.

MOM IN CHIEF

In addition to her many duties as First Lady, Michelle Obama also keeps busy taking care of Malia and Sasha. She spends time with her daughters whenever she can, attending Saturday soccer matches, looking over homework assignments, and arranging slumber parties, after-school activities, and playdates.

DADDY DUTIES

In addition to all of his responsibilities as the U.S. head of state, Barack Obama is also a father. He makes sure to be around for the important moments in his daughters' lives. Just like other dads, he attends their sports matches and teacher conferences. Sometimes, when Malia and Sasha can accompany their parents on a trip, the whole family even gets to do a little sightseeing together.

President Obama and Malia share a laugh as they get into the presidential limo on their way to Sasha's school, where the President will have a parent-teacher conference.

President Obama cheers for
Sasha's soccer team.

BUSY DAYS
ON THE ROAD

PRESIDENT OBAMA IS CONSTANTLY ON THE MOVE. To keep up with the American people, he travels around the country, delivering speeches, touring schools and factories, giving interviews, and hosting town hall meetings. For discussions about international relations, he goes to conferences abroad. And sometimes, between hectic weeks of work, the President finds time to spend weekends away from the White House with his family. Read on to learn more about the President's travels and the high-tech vehicles that take him across the country and around the world.

4

TRAVELING AROUND THE COUNTRY

With Air Force One always at the ready, President Obama can visit people throughout the 50 states to learn about what is going on in their communities. Here are a few pages taken straight from the President's public calendar that show what he does when he's on the move in the United States.

FEBRUARY 17, 2009

9:25 A.M. Interview with members of the Canadian Broadcasting Corporation

9:40 A.M. Depart South Lawn aboard Marine One

10:00 A.M. Depart Andrews Air Force Base aboard Air Force One

1:30 P.M. Arrive in Aurora, Colorado

2:15 P.M. Tour solar-panel installation at the Denver Museum of Nature and Science

2:40 P.M. Deliver remarks and sign the American Recovery and Reinvestment Act

5:25 P.M. Depart Denver aboard Air Force One

7:05 P.M. Arrive in Phoenix, Arizona

MARCH 19, 2009

9:00 A.M. Receive President's Daily Briefing in Los Angeles, California

10:30 A.M. Tour Edison Electric Vehicle Technical Center Garage of the Future in Pomona, California

10:45 A.M. Deliver remarks about energy and eco-friendly vehicles at the Edison Electric Vehicle Technical Center

12:05 P.M. Depart Edison Electric Vehicle Technical Center

1:10 P.M. Hold town hall meeting with local residents at the Miguel Contreras Learning Center in Los Angeles. (California Governor Arnold Schwarzenegger, Los Angeles Mayor Antonio Villaraigosa, and Secretary of Labor Hilda Solis will be there.)

3:10 P.M. Depart Miguel Contreras Learning Center

4:20 P.M. Tape interview on The Tonight Show with Jay Leno in Burbank, California

5:50 P.M. Depart from the Long Beach Airport in California aboard Air Force One

MARCH 20, 2009

1:05 A.M. Arrive at Andrews Air Force Base

1:20 A.M. Arrive at the White House

APRIL 29, 2009

8:00 A.M. With Vice President Biden and Senator Arlen Specter, make a statement before the press in the Diplomatic Reception Room about Senator Arlen Specter's decision to change political parties and become a Democrat

8:15 A.M. Depart South Lawn aboard Marine One

8:30 A.M. Depart Andrews Air Force Base aboard Air Force One

10:30 A.M. Arrive in Saint Louis, Missouri

11:20 A.M. Hold town hall meeting at Fox High School and answer questions on the economy, health care, the environment, the wars in Iraq and Afghanistan, and other topics

2:00 P.M. Depart St. Louis aboard Air Force One

3:45 P.M. Arrive at Andrews Air Force Base

4:00 P.M. Arrive at the White House

8:00 P.M. Hold prime-time news conference in East Room and talk about first 100 days in office

PRESIDENTIAL EVENTS
AROUND THE U.S.

President Obama travels around the country for many reasons. One of the biggest reasons for him to tour the country is to communicate with citizens. In towns and cities big and small, the President hosts town hall meetings to speak about his vision for his presidency and get a sense of the issues facing his audiences.

Of course, the President isn't the only American who needs to get around the country. To help citizens travel with more ease, President Obama has proposed a national network of high-speed railroads. As Vice President Biden put it, "We're going to make travel in this country leaner and a whole lot cleaner."

President Obama holds a town hall meeting at Fox Senior High School in Arnold, Missouri.

Members of the audience asked the President questions about the automobile industry, retirement benefits, school improvement, and making the country more environmentally friendly.

PAST PRESIDENTS

As traveling long distances became easier, U.S. Presidents visited states farther and farther from the capital. **Rutherford B. Hayes** was the first sitting President to make it as far as California. Over a period of 71 days, he traveled by steamship, railroad, and stagecoach to get to the country's westernmost states. Because he moved around so much, he earned the nickname Rutherford the Rover. President Obama can now simply board Air Force One to get to California in a few hours.

TRAVELING AROUND THE WORLD

The President travels around the world to meet with other world leaders and attend important conferences. Take a look at a few pages of President Obama's calendar to learn more about how he spends his days outside of our country.

Barack Obama's February 2009 trip to Canada was his first trip abroad as President.

FEBRUARY 19, 2009

9:00 A.M. Depart South Lawn aboard Marine One

9:15 A.M. Depart Andrews Air Force Base on Air Force One

10:30 A.M. Arrive in Ottawa, Canada

10:50 A.M. Meet with Governor General of Canada, Michaëlle Jean, in the Canada Reception Centre at the Ottawa International Airport

11:40 A.M. Arrive at Parliament Hill, meet Prime Minister Stephen Harper and Parliament officials

11:45 A.M. Sign guest books

12:00 P.M. Meet with Prime Minister Harper in the Office of the Prime Minister

12:55 P.M. Working lunch with Prime Minister Harper

2:45 P.M. With Prime Minister Harper, speak to the press

4:00 P.M. Meet with Leader of the Official Opposition Michael Ignatieff

4:20 P.M. Meet with U.S. Embassy employees and family members

5:15 P.M. Depart Ottawa aboard Air Force One

6:40 P.M. Arrive at Andrews Air Force Base

7:00 P.M. Arrive at the White House

Barack Obama's first overseas trip as President was to London for the G-20, or Group of Twenty, Summit. There, leaders of the most powerful nations in the world met to discuss the global financial system.

APRIL 1, 2009

8:05 A.M. Meet privately with British Prime Minister Gordon Brown at 10 Downing Street in London

9:00 A.M. Hold expanded meeting with Prime Minister Brown

10:15 A.M. Hold a press conference with Prime Minister Brown at the Foreign and Commonwealth Office Building

11:45 A.M. Meet with Russian leaders at Winfield House, the home of the U.S. Ambassador to the United Kingdom

1:00 P.M. Meet with David Cameron, the Conservative party leader in Britain, at Winfield House

2:00 P.M. Meet with Chinese leaders at Winfield House

5:35 P.M. With First Lady, have private audience with Queen Elizabeth II at Buckingham Palace

6:00 P.M. With First Lady, attend G-20 leaders reception at Buckingham Palace

8:30 P.M. Attend G-20 working dinner at Winfield House

APRIL 6, 2009

10:50 A.M. Attend wreath-laying ceremony at Anitkabir, the memorial tomb of Mustafa Kemal Atatürk, Turkey's first president, in Ankara, Turkey.

11:55 A.M. Meet one-on-one with Turkish President Abdullah Gul

12:20 P.M. Hold bilateral meeting with President Gul

1:45 P.M. With President Gul, make a statement to the press

3:30 P.M. Address Turkish Grand National Assembly at Turkish Parliament

4:25 P.M. Hold bilateral meeting with Prime Minister Recep Tayyip Erdogan

6:10 P.M. Depart Ankara

7:10 P.M. Arrive in Istanbul, Turkey

PRESIDENTIAL EVENTS AROUND THE WORLD

President Obama cannot conduct all of his important meetings from the White House. He often travels to other countries to see other heads of state. For example, Barack Obama has traveled to London to meet with leaders of other powerful nations and talk about improving the world economy. He also sat down with Russian President Dmitry Medvedev to talk about getting rid of stockpiles of nuclear weapons.

While in London, President Obama met with Chinese President Hu Jintao. The two leaders spoke about strengthening the relationship between the U.S. and China and working together in areas that could benefit both countries, including trade, law enforcement, science, and technology.

When the President and First Lady met with the Queen of England on April 1, 2009, they presented her with a rare autographed American songbook and an iPod filled with some hit Broadway tunes and video footage of one of her previous U.S. visits. The Queen gave the Obamas a framed portrait of herself and the Duke of Edinburgh.

The President and his advisers tour the Pyramids at Giza with Egyptian officials.

Heads of state often give one another gifts during their visits. These presents are symbols of goodwill and friendship from one leader to another. When the Obamas were in London, they gave Britain's prime minister, Gordon Brown, a DVD collection of classic American films. The First Lady then gave models of Marine One, the presidential helicopter, to Brown's sons. The Browns gave Malia and Sasha dresses and jewelry, as well as a set of books by English authors.

PAST PRESIDENTS

The first U.S. President to visit a foreign country was **Theodore Roosevelt.** In November 1906, President Roosevelt traveled to Panama City to see the construction of the Panama Canal. An incredibly difficult project, the canal was built to connect the Atlantic and Pacific Oceans. Before the Panama Canal opened in 1914, ships had to travel an extra 8,000 miles (12,875 km) around the southern tip of South America to get from one ocean to the other.

A doctor is always on Air Force One in case of a medical emergency.

Unlike most commercial planes, Air Force One has its own staircase. This way, the President does not need to rely on stairs with wheels that may not fit or might cause delays or security issues.

AIR FORCE ONE

When the President travels long distances, he usually flies aboard one of two Boeing 747-200B aircrafts that have been made especially to carry the U.S. head of state. These planes, which are both called Air Force One, have the most up-to-date communications and security technology. On board, there are 87 phone lines—and 28 of them are completely secure for top-secret conversations. Because it can refuel while it is still in the air, Air Force One can travel any distance. It can travel at speeds up to 700 miles (1,127 km) per hour.

PAST PRESIDENTS

After the assassination of President John F. Kennedy in 1963, **Lyndon Johnson** was sworn in as President aboard Air Force One at Love Field in Dallas, Texas. Federal judge Sarah Hughes administered the oath of office, while **First Lady Jackie Kennedy** looked on. President Johnson placed his hand on a Catholic prayer book during the short ceremony because a Bible could not be found aboard Air Force One.

A Mini White House in the Sky

President Obama relaxes aboard Air Force One.

Air Force One is nearly as tall as a six-story building. There are three levels to the plane, but the middle floor is where most of the action takes place. Here, the President has a bedroom, bathroom, offices, and even a place to work out. There is an area for staff to work and another area for reporters that are traveling with the President. Seventy passengers can comfortably fit on board, along with the 26-person crew. (A commercial 747 is set up to carry 250 people.) The plane's kitchen can serve up to 100 people at one time.

Air Force One is fully capable of serving as a mobile command unit in the event of an emergency on the ground. It is so well equipped that some refer to it as the flying White House.

UNITED STA

Members of the Air Force salute the presidential plane. Decorated with an American flag, the presidential seal, and the words "United States of America," Air Force One is a visible symbol of the U.S. presidency anywhere in the world.

DID YOU KNOW?

Technically, any Air Force jet that is carrying the President of the United States is referred to as Air Force One. If the President flies in an Army aircraft, that plane is known as Army One as long as he is on board.

Whenever the President exits Marine One, he is met by a ceremonial guard.

MARINE ONE

Flying in a helicopter is one of the easiest ways to move the President from one location to another nearby. It can be much simpler than moving the President by car, which might end up with the President stuck in traffic or require advance teams to close roads to other drivers. The presidential helicopter, known as Marine One, often picks up the President, along with his family or advisers, from the South Lawn of the White House. A short flight in Marine One can take the President from the White House to Air Force One, which is generally kept at Andrews Air Force Base in Maryland.

TIME *for* **Fun**

The first time the Obamas flew together on Marine One, the President said he was impressed by the amazing view of Washington, D.C. He joked that Malia and Sasha were more interested in the number of jars of candy kept on board for them.

Marine One always flies with several other identical helicopters to keep people from knowing exactly which aircraft carries the President.

President Obama and his family return home from Camp David aboard Marine One. Here, the helicopter and its decoys can be seen flying over the Jefferson Memorial.

THE PRESIDENT'S LIMO

When the President travels by car, he rides in a limousine that is usually surrounded by a group of other cars, police cruisers, Secret Service vehicles, motorcycles, an ambulance, and several SUVs. A special, highly secure Cadillac limousine was designed and created for President Obama. Called Cadillac One, it came into service for President Obama's inauguration on January 20, 2009.

When the President is away from the White House, a presidential car is flown to his location so he can always travel in a secure automobile.

TIME for Fun

First Lady Michelle Obama likes to joke about how huge the presidential motorcade is. In an interview with talk show host Oprah Winfrey, she said, "There were like 20 cars! There was everything in that motorcade except the caboose! Now I tease Barack: 'You've got the horse and carriage, the dog sled, the airplane, the bike…'"

There are two flags displayed on the front of the presidential limo. When the President is in the United States, the U.S. flag and the presidential standard can be seen. While traveling abroad, the U.S. flag and the flag of the country the President is visiting are flown.

The President's limo is parked outside Buckingham Palace in London, England.

The President never has to worry about flat tires. There are solid wheels underneath the rubber so the car won't be slowed down even if the tires are pierced.

PAST PRESIDENTS

William McKinley was the first U.S. President to ride in an automobile, but it was not an official government vehicle. **Teddy Roosevelt** was the first President to be driven around in a government-owned car. In 1921, Warren Harding became the first U.S. head of state to ride to his inaugural ceremony in a car.

The windows of Cadillac One are made from glass so thick that it blocks out most of the light from the outside.

DID ★ YOU ★ KNOW?

The President's limo is nicknamed the Beast.

A BUNKER ON WHEELS

Cadillac One was built with many up-to-date security precautions. For example, it is armor-plated and has 8-inch-thick (20-cm) doors. The underside of the car is protected by 5 inches (13 cm) of steel plating. When the doors are closed, the car is sealed so that no air comes in and little outside noise can be heard. Cadillac One has its own air supply, night vision cameras, and other top-secret security features.

Often the roads that the presidential motorcade will be taking are closed to all other traffic. Here the empty streets of Istanbul are surrounded by Turkish police as President Obama and his motorcade drive past.

Security agents take up their positions on the roof of Sasha's school while the President and First Lady are inside for a teacher conference.

THE U.S. SECRET SERVICE

Being President is a big job. And so is keeping the President safe. Whether the President is meeting with a senator or heading to a soccer match, the Secret Service is there, both in uniform and everyday clothes. These men and women are responsible for searching buildings, hotels, and meeting places before the President arrives to make sure they are secure. There are approximately 3,200 special agents, 1,300 uniformed officers, and more than 2,000 other people all working together to keep President Obama, his family, and senior members of the administration out of harm's way.

During speeches and other events that involve large crowds, agents keep their eyes peeled for anything unusual. They check the roads along the presidential motorcade's route and always know the quickest and safest ways to get the President out of any building or situation.

DID ★ YOU ★ KNOW?

During the 2008 Presidential campaign, the Secret Service gave each member of the Obama family a code name. They referred to the President-elect as Renegade. Michelle Obama was called Renaissance, and Malia and Sasha were known as Rosebud and Radiance.

THE SECRET SERVICE'S OTHER JOB

One of the oldest law enforcement agencies in the country, the Secret Service was founded in 1865. At the time, it was a branch of the U.S. Treasury Department. Originally, the agency investigated **counterfeiting**, which is the creation of fake money. It was not until President William McKinley was assassinated in 1901 that the Secret Service took on the role it is known for today. (The agency still investigates counterfeiting and other money-related crimes like credit card fraud and bank robberies.)

DID ★ YOU ★ KNOW?

The Secret Service also protects Presidents-elect, Vice Presidents-elect, former Presidents and their spouses, children of former Presidents until they reach age 16, important visitors, and official U.S. representatives traveling abroad.

Members of the U.S. Secret Service keep watch as President Obama participates in a national service project.

President Obama meets troops during a surprise trip to Iraq. He told them "You have given Iraq the opportunity to stand on its own as a democratic country."

SURPRISE!

Just about everything the President does each day is planned far in advance and down to the minute. But sometimes, for security reasons, the public doesn't know where the commander in chief will show up.

On April 7, 2009, after President Obama finished a successful tour of Europe, he hopped aboard Air Force One for a surprise visit with the troops in Iraq. He landed at Baghdad International Airport under heavy security and met with General Ray Odierno, the top U.S. military commander in Iraq. He also met with Iraqi leaders. While in Baghdad, the President spoke before a group of 600 troops.

President Obama isn't the only one to cause a sensation wherever he goes. First Lady Michelle Obama also gets in on the act. One day, President Obama and the First Lady took a break from their busy workdays to drop by a nearby school. What was the reason for stopping by? President Obama told the children, "We were just tired of being in the White House."

UNPLANNED VISITS

U.S. troops are not the only ones who've been shocked by a visit from the U.S. head of state. As President, it isn't easy for Barack Obama to just show up at a local restaurant or shop. His Secret Service agents need time and planning to make sure an area is safe. But that doesn't mean the President can never stray from his schedule.

After meeting with Canadian Prime Minister Stephen Harper in Ottawa, Canada, the presidential motorcade made an unannounced pit stop at a well-known farmers' market.

He has also shocked customers at restaurants, shops, and other public places when he drops by unexpectedly.

President Obama can even surprise people in his own house. All he has to do is pop into the White House press area, flower shop, or kitchen.

President Obama picked up Canadian sweets and souvenirs for Malia and Sasha.

WEEKEND GETAWAYS

The President may work longer hours than the average person and his tasks may be a bit more difficult, but just like everyone else, sometimes he likes to gather up the family and go away for the weekend. The Obamas relocated to Washington, D.C., for their role as First Family, so when they want to get away from it all, most often, they go back to Chicago, Illinois.

To get from Washington, D.C., to Chicago, the Obamas are flown on Air Force One to Chicago's O'Hare International Airport, then they take a short ride aboard Marine One to land closer to their home in the neighborhood of Kenwood. Finally, they are driven to their house in the presidential limo.

HOME AWAY FROM HOME

The Secret Service arrives early and sets up a safe area around the home in Kenwood. No parking is allowed on the streets within that area, and people must present identification to show that they live or work there in order to get past security. Neighbors are also told which streets they may walk down and which streets are off-limits.

The Obamas also make regular weekend trips to nearby Camp David, a scenic country retreat in Maryland's Catoctin Mountains. (For more on Camp David, see p. 106.)

The Obamas arrive at the airport in Chicago.

Spotlight

MARIAN ROBINSON

Though there are many staff members in the White House who make the Obamas' lives easier, there is one woman they swear they can't live without. At 71 years of age, Marian Robinson, the First Lady's mother, moved to Washington to help look after Malia and Sasha. After working for many years as a bank manager, Mrs. Robinson retired to help with her grandchildren during the presidential campaign. Now as First Grandma, she is able to take the girls to school, check their homework, and tuck them in when their parents can't be around. And when the family takes a break for the weekend, Marian Robinson is right there with them.

The President and First Lady walk toward Marine One, which will take them to Camp David.

PRESIDENTIAL RETREAT

About 70 miles (113 km) from Washington, D.C., in Maryland's scenic Catoctin Mountains is a weekend house known as Camp David. Since 1942, U.S. Presidents have been using this as a retreat, and President Obama and his family are no different. The Obamas take regular trips to Camp David to unwind. With a pool, tennis courts, and many hiking trails and paths, the retreat offers plenty of activities for the First Family and their guests to enjoy.

DID YOU KNOW?

President Franklin D. Roosevelt named the retreat Shangri-La. In 1953, President Eisenhower renamed the area Camp David after his grandson.

President Carter and the leaders of Isreal and Egypt (Prime Minister Begin and President Sadat) discuss the Camp David peace accords in 1978.

President and Mrs. Ford enjoy a relaxing weekend with their daughter, Susan.

In 1973, President Nixon chats with Soviet leader Leonid Brezhnev.

TIME CAPSULE:
CAMP DAVID

Some Presidents have used Camp David as a place to enjoy the quiet and to spend time with their families surrounded by nature. Others have used the retreat as a place to get work done. President Dwight Eisenhower was the first U.S. leader to hold a Cabinet meeting at Camp David.

In 1978, President Jimmy Carter famously hosted Israeli Prime Minister Menachem Begin and Egyptian President Anwar al-Sadat at the presidential retreat. Together, they made an important Middle East peace agreement. Here are a few moments in the history of Camp David.

During the Vietnam War, President Lyndon Johnson uses Camp David as a quiet place to meet with the U.S. ambassador to South Vietnam.

President Kennedy and his children, John Jr. and Caroline, take advantage of the great outdoors.

GOOD NIGHT, MR. PRESIDENT

THE PRESIDENT'S EVENING SCHEDULE can be as busy as his daytime appointment book, or it can include a quiet dinner with his family. Read on to learn more about the events inside and outside the White House that take up the President's time once the sun has gone down.

FAMILY TIME

Whenever he can, President Obama likes to share dinner with his family. During their evening meals, the First Family has a tradition they refer to as "Thorns and Roses." They will go around the table, telling one another about something good and something bad that happened during their day. The good events are roses and the unpleasant ones are thorns. The game helps the family stay up to date on the things that happen to them day to day. It gives them a chance to celebrate their joys together and also a chance to talk about how to deal with difficult situations.

Once, after the President told his family about a particularly rough day, Malia responded, "You have a really thorny job." In an interview with *People* magazine, Michelle Obama said, "I have to say, I've had a lot of rosy days. I think I have the good end of the deal."

AFTER-DINNER TREATS

Malia and Sasha go to bed much earlier than their parents, but sometimes they attend the awesome evening events at the White House. For example, the Obama girls got front row seats to the first-ever White House poetry jam. The performers included actor James Earl Jones; writers Michael Chabon and Ayelet Waldman; and jazz musicians Esperanza Spalding and Eric Lewis. The President introduced the evening, saying, "We're here to celebrate the power of words."

Malia and Sasha stayed up late and joined their parents in the East Room for an evening of poetry, music, and literature.

JOut on the Town

ust because he has a country to run doesn't mean the President is always working. Sometimes he enjoys his downtime outside of the White House bubble. He and the First Lady like going to the theater or sharing dinners. Other nights, they attend events such as the annual White House Correspondents' Dinner or the gala to honor Abraham Lincoln's memory at Ford's Theater.

A huge basketball fan, President Obama squeezes in a game from time to time. Here he watches the Washington Wizards beat his hometown team, the Chicago Bulls.

President and Mrs. Obama attend a dance performance at the John F. Kennedy Center for the Performing Arts. Known as the Kennedy Center, this theater hosts many dance, music, and opera companies.

HOST WITH THE MOST

Due to security concerns, it is often easier for the President to socialize in his own home than attend parties elsewhere. Luckily, the beautiful decor and the talented staff of the White House make it easy to host parties and events.

President Obama had been in office less than two weeks when he threw a Super Bowl party in the East Wing of the White House. He and the First Lady have begun a tradition of Wednesday evening get-togethers, to which they invite members of Congress from both political parties. They have also held a number of other gatherings, from small, private celebrations to huge daylong events like the Easter Egg Roll on the White House lawn, which is open to the public.

First Lady Michelle Obama has proven her skill at being a hostess. Here, she hosts one of a series of events in honor of women's history month.

The President and First Lady try out 3-D glasses during a Super Bowl half-time show.

Spotlight

PAST PRESIDENTS

U.S. Presidents have always invited the public to the presidential mansion for one reason or another. One of the strangest invitations was from President Andrew Jackson. In 1837, a dairy farmer from New York sent an enormous gift to the President: a **1,400-pound** (635-kg) **wheel of cheese**. The President left the cheese in the entrance hall and invited the public to come and help themselves. Visitors eventually ate it all, but the stain and stink it left behind lasted a long time.

President and Mrs. Obama host a seder in the White House for family and friends. A seder is a special ceremonial dinner held during the Jewish holiday Passover.

DESIREE ROGERS

The President and First Lady have a lot of behind-the-scenes help in staging an event. That's where Desiree Rogers comes in. As White House social secretary, she is responsible for organizing fancy state dinners, meals with groups of congressmen and women, and gatherings like poetry slams and movie nights. Rogers is the first African American to have the job of social secretary. She wants to find more ways to include average Americans in the events at the White House and is working on a lottery system used for choosing these special guests.

COOKING IN THE WHITE HOUSE

The duties of the kitchen staff change constantly depending on the White House schedule of events. A great deal of work goes into developing menus, connecting with local food suppliers and the on-site gardeners, organizing the cooking and serving staff, and planning every detail of each meal, from the appetizers to the desserts and from the china to the flowers. For example, it took the kitchen staff two days to organize and cook one fancy meal for 130 guests.

Cristeta Comerford is the White House's executive chef. She stays mighty busy making sure that the First Family is well-fed and that memorable menus are created for White House guests. There are usually seven people on the kitchen staff plus two full-time pastry chefs, but when a meal is being prepared for a big event, she invites other cooks to help.

DID★YOU★KNOW?

A White House carpenter with an interest in beekeeping has installed two beehives on the grounds. Now there is always fresh honey in the presidential kitchen.

In the White House kitchen, Social Secretary Desiree Rogers and the First Lady join a group of students who are studying to be chefs. They get to try out the food that will be served at a formal dinner in the State Room.

Cristeta Comerford is the first female executive chef at the White House. Born and raised in the Philippines, she moved to the United States in 1985.

THE WHITE HOUSE KITCHEN

Compared to the huge kitchens found in large hotels or catering halls, the main White House kitchen is fairly small. It is about 22 feet x 17.5 feet (7 m x 5 m), including its pantry. "This is where the magic happens. No one would expect that all that comes out of these dinners happens in this little bitty space," Mrs. Obama says.

The White House chefs are pleased with the First Lady's organic garden, which provides them with fresh herbs and veggies such as spinach, broccoli, kale, onion, lettuce, carrots, and radishes.

ADDRESSING THE NATION

Once a year, the President speaks before a joint session of the legislature and shares with members of government and the public his thoughts on how the country is doing. This speech, known as the State of the Union address, is generally delivered at the end of January. In inaugural years, the President does not deliver a State of the Union. Instead, he gives an important address to Congress reflecting his recommendations for the near future.

President Obama addresses Congress on the evening of February 24, 2009.

In President Obama's first address before a joint session of Congress, he assured the American people that the country would recover from the economic crisis and asked Congress to work with his administration to jump-start the economy, invest in schools, reduce the dependence on oil for energy, and bring down the high cost of health care.

PAST PRESIDENTS

George Washington delivered the nation's first State of the Union speech in New York City on January 8, 1790.

IN THE NEWS

In addition to giving speeches and holding press conferences, President Obama keeps Americans up to date on what's going on with the government through the White House Web site. His weekly video address and the White House blog are both available online at whitehouse.gov. Obama also gives interviews to newspapers, magazines, TV shows, and Web sites.

To show a lighter side of himself, he has appeared on news shows such as *60 Minutes* and talk shows. With a March 2009 appearance on *The Tonight Show with Jay Leno*, he became the first U.S. President to be a guest on a late-night comedy show while in office. On the show, he joked that in Washington, "It's a little bit like *American Idol*, except everybody is Simon Cowell."

President Obama conducts interviews with members of the press in the White House Map Room.

DID★YOU★KNOW?

Barack Obama's first television interview after becoming President was on an Arabic news station called Al-Arabiya. He told them, "I cannot respect terrorist organizations that would kill innocent civilians, and we will hunt them down. But to the broader Muslim world, what we are going to be offering is a hand of friendship."

WORKING LATE

According to President Obama, one of the biggest perks of the job is that he can see Malia and Sasha in the evenings—even if he still has more work to do. In a February 2009 interview, he said: "I can have dinner with them, I can help them with their homework, I can tuck them in. If I've got to go back to the office, I can."

Malia and Sasha are expected to be in bed at 8 P.M., but the President and First Lady stay up later than that, working or catching up with each other.

DID YOU KNOW?

When President Obama told a reporter that he was reading *Netherland* by the Irish author Joseph O'Neill, the sales of the book jumped dramatically. Many people want to read what the President is reading.

HEADING HOME

President Obama admits he's a night owl. He has been known to stay in the office till 10 P.M., working or reading newspapers. Then, he'll head back to the Residence and continue pouring over work until around midnight. When the President has had enough of all of the briefings that he reads every day, he curls up in bed with a novel. Then, he's off to sleep, getting some rest before he wakes up and starts another busy day as President of the United States.

TEST YOUR PRESIDENTIAL IQ

To stay on top of the nation's top job, President Obama must read a lot and remember what he's read. Can you? Put your brain to the test and see how much you've picked up from *TIME For Kids President Obama*.

Put a ✔ by the correct answer or fill in the blank.

1. What job did Barack Obama have while he ran for President?

❏ U.S. Senator

❏ U.S. Representative

❏ Illinois state senator

❏ University of Chicago professor

2. Which of these rooms does NOT exist in the White House?

❏ The Oval Office

❏ The Cabinet Room

❏ The East Room

❏ The Bill-Signing Hall

3. What is it called when the President refuses to sign a bill into law?

_____

4. What is the nickname of the Presidential limo?

❏ The Dinosaur

❏ The Beast

❏ The Monster

❏ The Lizard

5. What government agency is responsible for breaking codes?

❏ The Central Intelligence Agency

❏ The Supreme Court

❏ The National Security Agency

❏ The Department of the Interior

6. What is the name of the President's mountaintop retreat in Maryland?

❏ Camp Susan

❏ Camp Sunshine

❏ Camp David

❏ Camp Dolores

7. What is the name of the Obamas' dog?

_____

8. How many bathrooms are there in the White House?

❏ 1

❏ 6

❏ 35

❏ 102

9. What does the Secret Service do?

❏ Protect the President and his family

❏ Protect former Presidents and their spouses

❏ Investigate crimes involving U.S. money

❏ All of the above

10. What addition has First Lady Michelle Obama made to the White House?

❏ Installed a bowling alley

❏ Planted a vegetable garden

❏ Built a doghouse

❏ Redesigned the Oval Office

11. What special guests surprised Malia and Sasha Obama on Inauguration Day?

_____

12. The President has many duties. Which of these is NOT part of the President's job?

❏ Serving as commander in chief of the U.S. armed forces

❏ Delivering the State of the Union address every year

❏ Designing and printing U.S. money

❏ Appointing Supreme Court justices and Cabinet members

13. What is the President's favorite sport?

_____

Answers on page 128.

INDEX

PHOTO CREDITS

ANSWERS:

Page: 39:

Look out behind you
Top Secret
Enter at your own risk

Page 124–125:

1. U.S. Senator
2. The Bill-Signing Hall
3. A veto
4. The Beast
5. The National Security Agency
6. Camp David
7. Bo
8. 35
9. All of the above
10. Planted a vegetable garden
11. Jonas Brothers
12. Designing and printing U.S. money
13. Basketball